Microsoft Excel 2016 Keyboard Shortcuts

For Windows

By

U. C-Abel Books.

All Rights Reserved

First Edition: 2016

ISBN-13:978-1533598820
ISBN-10: 1533598827

Published by U. C-Abel Books.

Table of Contents

Acknowledgement.

U. C-Abel Books will not take all the credits for Microsoft Excel 2016 keyboard shortcuts listed in this book, but shares it with Microsoft Corporation because some of the shortcut keys came from them and are "used with permission from Microsoft".

Dedication

This book is dedicated to computer users and lovers of keyboard shortcuts all over the world.

Introduction.

We enjoy using shortcut keys because they set us on a high plane that astonishes people around us when we work with them. As wonderful shortcuts users, the worst eyesore we witness in computing is to see somebody sluggishly struggling to execute a task through mouse usage when in actual sense shortcuts will help to save that person the time wasted. Most people have asked us to help them with a list of shortcut keys that can make them work as smartly as we do and that drove us into research to broaden our knowledge and truly help them as they demanded, that is the reason for the existence of this book. It is a great tool for lovers of shortcuts, and those who want to join the group.

Most times, the things we love don't come by easily. It is our love for keyboard shortcuts that made us to bear long sleepless nights like owls, just to make sure we get the best out of it, and it is the best we got that we are sharing with you in this book. You cannot be the same at computing after reading this book. The time you entrusted to our care is an expensive possession and we promise not to mess it up.

Thank you.

What to Know Before You Begin.

General Notes.

1. It is important to note that when using shortcuts to perform any command, you should make sure the target area is active, if not, you may get a wrong result. Example, if you want to highlight all texts, you must make sure the text field is active and if an object, make sure the object area is active. The active area is always known by the location where the cursor of your computer blinks.

2. Most of the keyboard shortcuts you will see in this book refer to the U.S. keyboard layout. Keys for other layouts might not correspond exactly to the keys on a U.S. keyboard.

3. The plus (+) signs that come in the middle of keyboard shortcuts simply mean the keys are meant to be combined or held down together not to be added as one of the shortcut keys. In a case where plus sign is needed; it will be duplicated (++).

4. For keyboard shortcuts in which you press one key immediately followed by another key, the keys are separated by a comma (,).

5. It is also important to note that the shortcut keys listed in this book are for Microsoft Excel 2016.

Short Forms Used in This Book and Their Full Meaning.

The following are short forms of keyboard shortcuts used in this Microsoft Excel 2016 Keyboard Shortcuts book and their full meaning.

1. Alt   -   Alternate Key
2. Caps Lock   -   Caps Lock Key
3. Ctrl   -   Control Key
4. Esc   -   Escape Key
5. F   -   Function Key
6. Num Lock   -   Number Lock Key
7. Shft   -   Shift Key
8. Tab   -   Tabulate Key
9. Win   -   Windows logo key
10. Prt sc   -   Print Screen

CHAPTER 1.

Gathering The Basic Knowledge Of Keyboard Shortcuts.

Without the existence of the keyboard, there wouldn't have been anything like keyboard shortcuts, so in this chapter we will learn a little about keyboard before moving to keyboard shortcuts.

1. Definition of Computer Keyboard.
This is an input device that is used to send data to the computer memory.

Sketch of a Keyboard

1.1 Types of Keyboard.

   i. Standard (Basic) Keyboard.
   ii. Enhanced (Extended) Keyboard.

i. **Standard Keyboard:** This is a keyboard designed during the 1800s for mechanical typewriters with just 10 function keys (F keys) placed at the left side of it.

ii. **Enhanced Keyboard:** This is the current 101 to 102-key keyboard that is included in almost all the personal computers (PCs) of nowadays, which has 12 function keys at the top side of it.

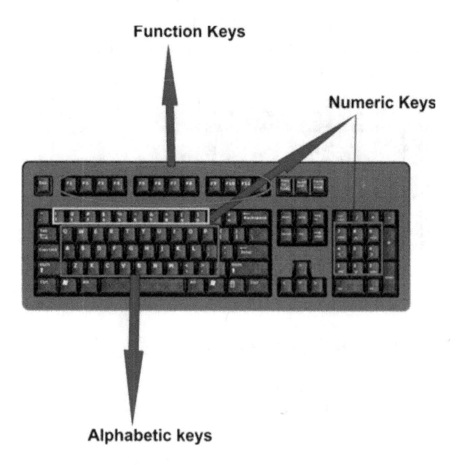

1.2 Segments of the keyboard

- Numeric keys
- Alphabetic keys
- Punctuation keys
- Windows Logo key.
- Function keys
- Special keys

Numeric Keys: Numeric keys are keys with numbers from **0 - 9**.

Alphabetic Keys: These are keys that have alphabets on them, ranging from **A-Z**.

Punctuation Keys: These are keys of the keyboard used for punctuation. Examples include comma, full stop, colon, question marks, hyphen etc.

Windows Logo Key: A key on Microsoft Computer keyboard with its logo displayed on it. Search for this ⊞ on your keyboard.

Function Keys: These are keys that have **F** on them which are usually combined with other keys. They are F1 - F12, and are also in the class called Special Keys.

Special Keys: These are keys that perform special functions. They include: Tab, Ctrl, Caps lock, Insert,

Prt sc, alt gr, Shift, Home, Num lock, Esc and many others. Special keys work according to the type of computer involved. In some keyboard layout, especially laptops, the keys that turn the speaker on/off, the one that increases/decreases volume, the key that turns the computer Wifi on/off are also special keys.

Other Special Keys Worthy of Note.

Enter Key: This is located at the right-hand corner of the keyboard. It is used to send messages to the computer to execute commands, in most cases it is used to mean "Ok" or "Go".

Escape Key (ESC): This is the first key on the upper left of the keyboard. It is used to cancel routines, close menus and select options such as **Save** according to circumstance.

Control Key (CTRL): It is located on the bottom row of the left and right hand side of the keyboard. They also work with the function keys to execute commands using Keyboard shortcuts (key combinations).

Alternate Key (ALT): It is located on the bottom row, very close to the CTRL key on both side of the keyboard. It enables many editing functions to be accomplished by using some keystroke combinations on the keyboard.

Shift Key: This adds to the functions of the function keys. In addition, it enables the use of alternative function of a particular button (key), especially, those with more than one function on a key. E.g. use of capital letters, symbols and numbers.

1.3. Selecting/Highlighting With the Keyboard.

This is a highlighting method or style where data is selected using the keyboard instead of a computer mouse.

To do this:

- Move your cursor to the text you want to highlight, make sure that area is active,
- Hold down the shift key with one finger
- Then use another finger to move the arrow key that points to the direction you want to highlight.

1.4 The Operating Modes Of The Keyboard.

Just like the mouse the keyboard has two operating modes. The two modes are Text Entering and Command Mode.

a.   **Text Entering Mode:** this mode gives the operator/user the opportunity to type text.

b. **Command Mode:** this is used to command the operating system/software/application to execute commands in certain ways.

2. Ways To Improve In Your Typing Skill.

1. Put Your Eyes Off The Keyboard.

This is the aspect of keyboard usage that many don't find funny because they always ask. "How can I put my eyes off the keyboard when I am running away from the occurrence of errors on my file?" My aim is to be fast, is this not going to slow me down?

Of course, there will be errors and at the same time your speed will slow down but the motive behind the introduction of this method is to make you faster than you are. Looking at your keyboard while you type can make you get a sore neck, it is better you learn to touch type because the more you type with your eyes fixed on the screen instead of the keyboard, the faster you become.

An alternative to keeping your eyes off your keyboard is to use the *"Das Keyboard Ultimate"*.

2. Errors Challenge You

It is better to fail than not to try at all. Not trying at all is an attribute of the weak and lazybones. When you make mistakes, try again because errors are opportunities for improvement.

3. Good Posture (Position Yourself Well).
Do not adopt an awkward position while typing. You should get everything on your desk organized or arranged before sitting to type. Your posture while typing contributes to your speed and productivity.

4. Practice
Here is the conclusion of everything said above. You have to practice your shortcuts constantly. The practice alone is a way of improvement. "Practice brings improvement". Practice always.

2.1 Software That Will Help You Improve In Your Typing Skill.

There are several Software programs for typing that both kids and adults can use for their typing skill. Here is a list of software that can help you improve in your typing: Mavis Beacon, Typing Instructor, Mucky Typing Adventure, Rapid Tying Tutor, Letter Chase Tying Tutor, Alice Touch Typing Tutor and many more. Personally, I recommend Mavis Beacon.

To learn typing with MAVIS BEACON, install Mavis Beacon software to your computer, start with keyboard lesson, then move to games. Games like **Penguin Crossing, Creature Lab** or **Space Junk** will help you become a professional in typing. Typing and keyboard shortcuts work hand-in-hand.

Sketch of a computer mouse

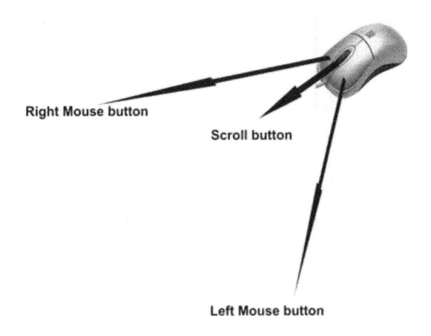

Right Mouse button

Scroll button

Left Mouse button

3. Mouse:

This is an oval-shaped portable input device with three buttons for scrolling, left clicking, and right clicking that enables work to be done effectively on a computer. The plural form of mouse is mice.

3.1 Types of Computer Mouse

- Mechanical Mouse
- Optical Mechanical Mouse (Optomechanical)
- Laser Mouse
- Optical Mouse

- BlueTrack Mouse

3.2 Forms of Clicking:

Left Clicking: This is the process of clicking the left side button of the mouse. It can be called *clicking* without the addition of *left*.

Right Clicking: It is the process of clicking the right side button of the mouse.

Double Clicking: It is the process of clicking the left side button two times (twice) and immediately.

Double clicking is used to select a word while thrice clicking is used to select a sentence or paragraph.

Scroll Button: It is the little key attached to the mouse that looks like a tiny wheel. It takes you up and down a page when moved.

3.3 Mouse Pad: This is a small soft mat that is placed under the mouse to make it have a free movement.

3.4 Laptop Mouse Touchpad

This unlike the mouse we explained above is not external, rather it is inbuilt (comes with a laptop computer). With the presence of a laptop mouse touchpad, an external mouse is not needed to use a laptop, except in a case where it is malfunctioning or the operator prefers to use external one for some reasons.

The laptop mouse touchpad is usually positioned at the end of the keyboard section of a laptop computer. It is rectangular in shape with two buttons positioned below it. The two buttons/keys are used for left and right clicking just like the external mouse. Some laptops come with four mouse keys. Two placed above the mouse for left and right clicking and two other keys placed below it for the same function.

4. Definition Of Keyboard Shortcuts.

Keyboard shortcuts are defined as a series of keys, sometimes with combination that execute tasks that typically involve the use of mouse or other input devices.

5. Why You Should Use Shortcuts.

1. One may not be able to use a computer mouse easily because of disability or pain.

2. One may not be able to see the mouse pointer as a result of vision impairment, in such case what will the person do? The answer is SHORTCUT.

3. Research has made it known that Extensive mouse usage is related to Repetitive Syndrome Injury (RSI) greatly than the use of keyboard.

4. Keyboard shortcuts speed up computer users, making learning them a worthwhile effort.

5. When performing a job that requires precision, it is wise that you use the keyboard instead of mouse, for instance, if you are dealing with Text Editing, it is better you handle it using keyboard shortcuts than spending more time with mouse alone.

6. Studies calculate that using keyboard shortcuts allows working 10 times faster than working with the mouse. The time you spend looking for the mouse and then getting the cursor to the position you want is lost! Reducing your work duration by 10 times brings you greater results.

5.1 Ways To Become A Lover Of Shortcuts.

1. Always have the urge to learn new shortcut keys associated with the programs you use.
2. Be happy whenever you learn a new shortcut.
3. Try as much as you can to apply the new shortcuts you learnt.
4. Always bear it in mind that learning new shortcuts is worth it.

5. Always remember that the use of keyboard shortcuts keeps people healthy while performing computing activities.

5.2 How To Learn New Shortcut Keys

1. Do a research for them: quick reference (a cheat sheet comprehensively compiled) can go a long way to help you improve.
2. Buy applications that show you keyboard shortcuts every time you execute an action with the mouse.
3. Disconnect your mouse if you must learn this fast.
4. Read user manuals and help topics (Whether offline or online).

5.3 Your Reward For Knowing Shortcut Keys.

1. You will get faster unimaginably.
2. Your level of efficiency will increase.
3. You will find it easy to use.
4. Opportunities are high that you will become an expert in what you do.
5. You won't have to go for **Office button**, click **New,** click **Blank and Recent** and click **Create** just to insert a fresh/blank page. **Ctrl +N** takes care of that in a second.

A Funny Note: Keyboard Shortcuts and Mousing are in a marital union with Keyboard Shortcuts being the head and it will be unfair for anybody to put asunder between them.

5.4 Why We Emphasize On The Use of Shortcuts.

You may never ditch your mouse completely unless you are ready to make your brain a box of keyboard shortcuts which will really be frustrating. Just imagine yourself learning all the shortcuts for the programs you use and its various versions. You shouldn't learn keyboard shortcuts that way.

Why we are emphasizing on the use of shortcuts is because mouse usage is becoming unusually common and unhealthy, too. So we just want to make sure both are combined so you can get fast, productive and healthy in your computing activities. All you need to know is just the most important ones associated with the programs you use.

CHAPTER 2.

15 (Fifteen) Special Keyboard Shortcuts.

The fifteen special keyboard shortcuts are fifteen (15) shortcut keys every computer user should know.

The following table contains the list of keyboard shortcuts every computer user should know.

1. **Ctrl + A:** Control plus A, highlights or selects everything you have in the environment where you are working.

    > *If you are like **"Wow, the content of this document is large and there is no time to select all of it, besides, it's going to mount pressure on my computer?"** Using the mouse for this is an outdated method of handling a task like selecting all, Ctrl+A will take care of that within seconds.*

2. **Ctrl + C:** Control plus C copies any highlighted or selected element within the work environment.

    > *Saves the time and stress which would have been used to right click and click again just to copy. Use ctrl+c.*

3. **Ctrl + N:** Control plus N opens a new window. *Instead of clicking* **File, New, blank/template** *and another* **click,** *just press* **Ctrl + N** *and a fresh window will appear instantly.*

4. **Ctrl + O:** Control plus O opens a new program. *Use ctrl +O when you want to locate or open a file or program.*

5. **Ctrl + P:** Control plus P prints the active document. *Always use this to locate the printer dialog box and print.*

6. **Ctrl + S:** Control plus S saves a new document or file and changes made by the user. *Going for the mouse? Please stop! Don't use the mouse. Just press Ctrl+S and everything will be saved.*

7. **Ctrl +V:** Control plus V pastes copied elements into the active area of the program in use. *Using ctrl+V in a case like this Saves the time and stress of right clicking and clicking again just to paste.*

8. **Ctrl + W:** Control plus W is used to close the page you are working on when you want to leave the work environment.

> *"There is a way Peace does this without using the mouse. Oh my God, why didn't I learn it then?"* Don't worry, I have the answer, Peace presses Ctrl+W to close active windows.

9. **Ctrl + X:** Control plus X cuts elements (making the elements to disappear from their original place). The difference between cutting and deleting elements is that in Cutting, what was cut doesn't get lost permanently but prepares itself so that it can be pasted in another location selected by the user.

> *Use ctrl+x when you think* ***"this shouldn't be here and I can't stand the stress of retyping or redesigning it in the rightful place it belongs".***

10. **Ctrl + Y:** Control plus Y redoes an undone action.

> *Ctrl+Z brought back what you didn't need? Press Ctrl+ Y to remove it again.*

11. **Ctrl + Z:** Control plus Z undoes actions.

Can't find what you typed now or a picture you inserted, it suddenly disappeared or you mistakenly removed it? Press Ctrl+Z to bring it back.

12. **Alt + F4:** Alternative plus F4 closes active windows or items.

   *You don't need to move the mouse in order to close an active window, just press **Alt + F4** if you are done or don't want somebody who is coming to see what you are doing.*

13. **Ctrl + F6:** Control plus F6 Navigates between open windows, making it possible for a user to see what is happening in windows that are active.
   Are you working in Microsoft Word and want to find out if the other active window where your browser is loading a page is still progressing? Use Ctrl + F6.

14. **F1:** This displays the help window.

   *Is your computer malfunctioning? Use **F1** to find help when you don't know what next to do.*

15. **F12:** This enables user to make changes to an already saved document.

F12 is the shortcut to use when you want to change the format in which you saved your existing document, password it, change its name, change the file location or destination, or make other changes to it. It will save your time.

CHAPTER 3.

Keyboard Shortcuts In Excel 2016.

Definition of Program: Microsoft Excel is an electronic spreadsheet program that enables its users to create, organize, format, and calculate data. It was first released for Macintosh in the year 1985 and later on released for Windows in 1987.

The following list contains keyboard shortcuts that will boost your productivity in Microsoft Excel.

Frequently Used Shortcuts.

TASK	SHORTCUT
Close a spreadsheet	Ctrl+W
Open a spreadsheet	Ctrl+O
Go to the **Home** tab	Alt+H
Save a spreadsheet	Ctrl+S
Copy	Ctrl+C
Paste	Ctrl+V
Undo	Ctrl+Z
Remove cell contents	Delete key
Choose a fill color	Alt+H, H
Cut	Ctrl+X
Go to **Insert** tab	Alt+N
Bold	Ctrl+B

Center align cell contents	Alt+H, A, then C
Go to **Page Layout** tab	Alt+P
Go to **Data** tab	Alt+A
Go to **View** tab	Alt+W
Format a cell from context menu	Shift+F10, or Context key
Add borders	Alt+H, B
Delete column	Alt+H,D, then C
Go to **Formula** tab	Alt+M

Keyboard Shortcuts To Navigate The Ribbon

The ribbon at the top of Excel 2016 groups related commands on tabs. For example, on the Home tab, the Number group includes the Number Format command.

You can navigate the ribbon using just the keyboard. Access keys are special shortcuts that let you quickly use a command on the ribbon by pressing a few keys. These access keys, called KeyTips, are visible when you press Alt or F10.

You can navigate the tabs in the ribbon as follows:

- To get to the ribbon, press Alt, and then, to move between tabs, use the Right Arrow and Left Arrow keys.

- To hide the ribbon so you have more room to work, press Ctrl+F1. Repeat to display the ribbon again.

Keyboard Shortcuts For SmartArt Graphics.

Insert a SmartArt graphic in an Office document

1. In the Microsoft Office program where you want to insert the graphic, press Alt, then N, and then M to open the **SmartArt Graphic** dialog box.
2. Press Up Arrow or Down Arrow to select the type of graphic that you want.
3. Press Tab to move to the Layout task pane.
4. Press the arrow keys to select the layout that you want.
5. Press Enter to insert the selected layout.

Work With Shapes In A SmartArt Graphic

TASK	SHORTCUT
Select the next element in a SmartArt graphic.	Tab
Select the previous element in a SmartArt graphic.	Shift+Tab
Select all shapes.	Ctrl +A
Remove focus from the selected shape.	Esc
Nudge the selected shape up.	Up Arrow

Nudge the selected shape down.	Down Arrow
Nudge the selected shape left.	Left Arrow
Nudge the selected shape right.	Right Arrow
Edit text in the selected shape.	Enter or F2, Esc to exit shape
Delete the selected shape.	Delete or Backspace
Cut the selected shape.	Ctrl+X or Shift+Delete
Copy the selected shape.	Ctrl+C
Paste the contents of the Clipboard.	Ctrl+V
Undo the last action.	Ctrl+Z

Move And Resize Shapes In A SmartArt Graphic

TASK	SHORTCUT
Enlarge the selected shape horizontally.	Shift+Right Arrow
Reduce the selected shape horizontally.	Shift+Left Arrow
Enlarge the selected shape vertically.	Shift+Up Arrow
Reduce the selected shape vertically.	Shift+Down Arrow
Rotate the selected shape to the right.	Alt+Right Arrow
Rotate the selected shape to the left.	Alt+Left Arrow

Notes:

- To apply more precise adjustments to shapes, press the Ctrl key in addition to any of the above keyboard shortcuts.
- These keyboard shortcuts apply to multiple selections as if you selected each item individually.

Work With Text In A SmartArt Graphic

TASK	SHORTCUT
Move one character to the left.	Left Arrow
Move one character to the right.	Right Arrow
Move up one line.	Up Arrow
Move down one line.	Down Arrow
Move one word to the left.	Ctrl+Left Arrow
Move one word to the right.	Ctrl+Right Arrow
Move one paragraph up.	Ctrl+Up Arrow
Move one paragraph down.	Ctrl+Down Arrow
Move to the end of a line.	End
Move to the beginning of a line.	Home
Move to the end of a text box.	Ctrl+End
Move to the beginning of a text box.	Ctrl+Home
Cut selected text.	Ctrl+X
Copy selected text.	Ctrl+C
Paste selected text.	Ctrl+V
Move the selected text up.	Alt+Shift+Up Arrow
Move the selected text down.	Alt+Shift+Down

	Arrow
Undo the last action.	Ctrl+Z
Delete one character to the left.	Backspace
Delete one word to the left.	Ctrl+Backspace
Delete one character to the right.	Delete
Delete one word to the right.	Ctrl+Delete
Promote the selected text.	Alt+Shift+Left Arrow
Demote the selected text.	Alt+Shift+Right Arrow
Check the spelling (not available in Word).	F7

Apply Character Formatting

TASK	SHORTCUT
Open the **Font** dialog box.	Ctrl+Shift+F or Ctrl+Shift+P
Increase the font size of the selected text.	Ctrl+Shift+>
Decrease the font size of the selected text.	Ctrl+Shift+<
Switch the case of selected text (lower case, Title Case, UPPER CASE).	Shift+F3
Apply bold formatting to the selected text.	Ctrl+B
Apply an underline to the selected text.	Ctrl+U
Apply italic formatting to the selected text.	Ctrl+I

Apply subscript formatting to the selected text.	Ctrl+Equal Sign
Apply superscript formatting to the selected text.	Ctrl+Shift+Plus Sign
Adjust the superscript/subscript offset up.	Ctrl+Alt+Shift+>
Adjust the superscript/subscript offset down.	Ctrl+Alt+Shift+<
Remove all character formatting from the selected text.	Shift+Ctrl+Spacebar

Copy Text Formatting

TASK	SHORTCUT
Copy formatting from the selected text.	Shift+Ctrl+C
Paste formatting to the selected text.	Shift+Ctrl+V

Apply Paragraph Formatting

TASK	SHORTCUT
Center a paragraph.	Ctrl+E
Justify a paragraph.	Ctrl+J
Left align a paragraph.	Ctrl+L
Right align a paragraph.	Ctrl+R
Demote a bullet point.	Tab or Alt+Shift+Right Arrow

Promote a bullet point.	Shift+Tab or Alt+Shift+Left Arrow

Use The Text Pane

TASK	SHORTCUT
Merge two lines of text.	Delete at the end of the first line of text
Display the shortcut menu.	Shift+F10
Switch between the **Text** pane and the drawing canvas.	Ctrl+Shift+F2
Close the **Text** pane.	Alt+F4
Switch the focus from the **Text** pane to the border of the SmartArt graphic.	Esc
Open the SmartArt graphics Help topic. (Your pointer should be in the Text pane.)	Ctrl +Shift+F1

□

Use The Keyboard To Work With The Ribbon.

Do tasks quickly without using the mouse by pressing a few keys—no matter where you are in an Office program. You can get to every command on the ribbon by using an access key—usually by pressing two to four keys.

1. Press and release the ALT key.

   You see the little boxes called KeyTips over each command available in the current view.

2. Press the letter shown in the KeyTip over the command you want to use.
3. Depending on which letter you pressed, you might see additional KeyTips. For example, if the **Home** tab is active and you pressed N, the **Insert** tab is displayed, along with the KeyTips for the groups in that tab.
4. Continue pressing letters until you press the letter of the specific command you want to use.

Tip: To cancel the action you're taking and hide the KeyTips, press and release the ALT key.

Change the keyboard focus without using the mouse

Another way to use the keyboard to work with the ribbon is to move the focus among the tabs and commands until you find the feature you want to use. The following shows some ways to move the keyboard focus without using the mouse.

TASK	SHORTCUT
Select the active tab and show the access keys.	ALT or F10. Press either of these keys again to move back to the Office file and cancel the access keys.
Move to another tab.	ALT or F10 to select the active tab, and then LEFT ARROW or RIGHT ARROW.
Move to another Group on	ALT or F10 to select the

the active tab.	active tab, and then CTRL+RIGHT ARROW or LEFT ARROW to move between groups.
Minimize (collapse) or restore the ribbon.	CTRL+F1
Display the shortcut menu for the selected item.	SHIFT+F10
Move the focus to select the active tab, your Office file, task pane, or status bar.	F6
Move the focus to each command in the ribbon, forward or backward.	ALT or F10, and then TAB or SHIFT+TAB
Move down, up, left, or right among the items in the ribbon.	DOWN ARROW, UP ARROW, LEFT ARROW, or RIGHT ARROW
Go to the selected command or control in the ribbon.	SPACE BAR or ENTER
Open the selected menu or gallery in the ribbon.	SPACE BAR or ENTER
Go to a command or option in the ribbon so you can change it.	ENTER
Finish changing the value of a command or option in the ribbon, and move focus back to the Office file.	ENTER
Get help on the selected	F1

command or control in the ribbon. (If no Help article is associated with the selected command, the Help table of contents for that program is shown instead.)	

Go To The Access Keys For The Ribbon.

To go directly to a tab on the ribbon, press one of the following access keys:

TASK	SHORTCUT
Open the Tell me box on the ribbon and type a search term for assistance or Help content.	Alt+Q, and then enter the search term.
Open the File page and use Backstage view.	Alt+F
Open the Home tab and format text and numbers and use the Find tool.	Alt+H
Open the Insert tab and insert PivotTables, charts, add-ins, Sparklines, pictures, shapes, headers, or text boxes.	Alt+N
Open the Page Layout tab and work with themes, page setup, scale, and alignment.	Alt+P
Open the Formulas tab and insert, trace, and customize functions and calculations.	Alt+M

Open the Data tab and connect to, sort, filter, analyze, and work with data.	Alt+A
Open the Review tab and check spelling, add comments, and protect sheets and workbooks.	Alt+R
Open the View tab and preview page breaks and layouts, show and hide gridlines and headings, set zoom magnification, manage windows and panes, and view macros.	Alt+W

Work In The Ribbon Tabs And Menus With The Keyboard.

When you switch the focus to a tab on the ribbon, or a context menu, you can then navigate within the tabs as follows:

TASK	SHORTCUT
Select the active tab of the ribbon, and activate the access keys.	Alt or F10. To move to a different tab, use access keys or the arrow keys.
Move the focus to commands on the ribbon.	Tab or Shift+Tab
Move down, up, left, or right, respectively, among the items on the ribbon.	The Down Arrow, Up Arrow, Left Arrow, or Right Arrow key
Activate a selected	Spacebar or Enter

button.	
Open the list for a selected command.	The Down Arrow key
Open the menu for a selected button.	Alt+Down Arrow
When a menu or submenu is open, move to the next command.	Down Arrow key
Expand or collapse the ribbon.	Ctrl+F1
Open a context menu.	Shift+F10 or Context key
Move to the submenu when a main menu is open or selected.	Left Arrow key

Use Access Keys When You Can See The KeyTips.

You can display KeyTips, which are the letters used to access commands, and then use them to navigate in the ribbon.

1. Press Alt. The KeyTips appear in small squares by each ribbon command.
2. To select a command, press the letter shown in the square KeyTip that appears by it.

Depending on which letter you press, you may be shown additional KeyTips. For example, if you press

Alt+F, Backstage view opens on the Info page, which has a different set of KeyTips. If you then press Alt again, KeyTips appear for navigating on the current page.

Will my old shortcuts work?

Keyboard shortcuts that begin with Ctrl still work in Excel 2016. For example, Ctrl+C still copies to the clipboard, and Ctrl+V still pastes from the clipboard. Most of the old Alt+ menu shortcuts still work, too. You just need to know the full shortcut from memory—there are no screen reminders of the letters to press. If you don't know the sequence, press Esc and use KeyTips instead.

Navigate In Cells: Keyboard Shortcuts.

TASK	SHORTCUT
Move to the previous cell in a worksheet or the previous option in a dialog box.	Shift+Tab
Move one cell up in a worksheet.	Up Arrow key
Move one cell down in a worksheet.	Down Arrow key
Move one cell left in a worksheet.	Left Arrow key
Move one cell right in a worksheet.	Right Arrow key
Move to the edge of the current data region in a worksheet.	Ctrl+arrow key
Enter End mode, move to the next nonblank cell in the same column or row as the active cell, and turn	End, arrow key

off End mode. If the cells are blank, move to the last cell in the row or column.	
Move to the last cell on a worksheet, to the lowest used row of the rightmost used column.	Ctrl+End
Extend the selection of cells to the last used cell on the worksheet (lower-right corner).	Ctrl+Shift+End
Move to the cell in the upper-left corner of the window when Scroll Lock is turned on.	Home+Scroll Lock
Move to the beginning of a row in a worksheet. Home Move to the beginning of a worksheet.	Ctrl+Home
Move one screen down in a worksheet.	Page Down
Move to the next sheet in a workbook.	Ctrl+Page Down
Move one screen to the right in a worksheet.	Alt+Page Down
Move one screen up in a worksheet.	Page Up
Move one screen to the left in a worksheet.	Alt+Page Up
Move to the previous sheet in a workbook.	Ctrl+Page Up
Move one cell to the right in a worksheet. Or, in a protected worksheet, move between unlocked cells.	Tab

Make Selections And Perform Actions: Keyboard Shortcuts

TASK	SHORTCUT
Select the entire worksheet.	Ctrl+A or Ctrl+Shift+Spacebar
Select the current and next sheet in a workbook.	Ctrl+Shift+Page Down
Select the current and previous sheet in a workbook.	Ctrl+Shift+Page Up
Extend the selection of cells by one cell.	Shift+arrow key
Extend the selection of cells to the last nonblank cell in the same column or row as the active cell, or if the next cell is blank, to the next nonblank cell.	Ctrl+Shift+arrow key
Turn extend mode on and use the arrow keys to extend a selection. Press again to turn off.	Turn extend mode on and use the arrow keys to extend a selection. Press again to turn off. F8
Add a non-adjacent cell or range to a selection of cells by using the arrow keys.	Shift+F8
Start a new line in the same cell.	Alt+Enter
Fill the selected cell	Ctrl+Enter

range with the current entry.	
Complete a cell entry and select the cell above.	Shift+Enter
Select an entire column in a worksheet.	Ctrl+Spacebar
Select an entire row in a worksheet.	Shift+Spacebar
Select all objects on a worksheet when an object is selected.	Ctrl+Shift+Spacebar
Extend the selection of cells to the beginning of the worksheet.	Ctrl+Shift+Home
Select the current region if the worksheet contains data. Press a second time to select the current region and its summary rows. Press a third time to select the entire worksheet.	Ctrl+A or Ctrl+Shift+Spacebar
Select the current region around the active cell or select an entire PivotTable report.	Ctrl+Shift+asterisk (*)
Select the first command on the menu when a menu or submenu is visible.	Home

Repeat the last command or action, if possible.	Ctrl+Y
Undo the last action.	Ctrl+Z

Format In Cells: Keyboard Shortcuts

TASK	SHORTCUT
Format a cell by using the Format Cells dialog box.	Ctrl+1
Format fonts in the Format Cells dialog box.	Ctrl+Shift+F or Ctrl+Shift+P
Edit the active cell and put the insertion point at the end of its contents. Or, if editing is turned off for the cell, move the insertion point into the formula bar. If editing a formula, toggle Point mode off or on so you can use arrow keys to create a reference.	F2
Add or edit a cell comment.	Shift+F2
Insert blank cells with the Insert dialog box.	Ctrl+Shift+Plus (+)
Display the Delete dialog box to delete selected cells.	Ctrl+Minus (-)
Enter the current time.	Ctrl+Shift+colon (:)

Enter the current date.	Ctrl+semi-colon (;)
Switch between displaying cell values or formulas in the worksheet.	Ctrl+grave accent (`)
Copy a formula from the cell above the active cell into the cell or the Formula Bar.	Ctrl+apostrophe (')
Move the selected cells.	Ctrl+X
Copy the selected cells.	Ctrl+C
Paste content at the insertion point, replacing any selection.	Ctrl+V
Paste content by using the Paste Special dialog box.	Ctrl+Alt+V
Italicize text or remove italic formatting.	Ctrl+I or Ctrl+3
Bold text or remove bold formatting.	Ctrl+B or Ctrl+2
Underline text or remove underline.	Ctrl+U or Ctrl+4
Apply or remove strikethrough formatting.	Ctrl+5
Switch between hiding objects, displaying objects, and displaying placeholders for objects.	Ctrl+6
Apply an outline border to the selected cells.	Ctrl+Shift+ampersand (&)
Remove the outline border from the selected cells.	Ctrl+Shift+underline (_)
Display or hide the	Ctrl+8

outline symbols.	
Hide the selected rows.	Ctrl+9
Hide the selected columns.	Ctrl+0
Use the Fill Down command to copy the contents and format of the topmost cell of a selected range into the cells below.	Ctrl+D
Use the Fill Right command to copy the contents and format of the leftmost cell of a selected range into the cells to the right.	Ctrl+R
Apply the General number format.	Ctrl+Shift+tilde (~)
Apply the Currency format with two decimal places (negative numbers in parentheses).	Ctrl+Shift+dollar sign ($)
Apply the Percentage format with no decimal places.	Ctrl+Shift+percent (%)
Apply the Scientific number format with two decimal places.	Ctrl+Shift+caret (^)
Apply the Date format with the day, month, and year.	Ctrl+Shift+number sign (#)
Apply the Time format with the hour and minute,	Ctrl+Shift+at sign (@)

and AM or PM.	
Apply the Number format with two decimal places, thousands separator, and minus sign (-) for negative values.	Ctrl+Shift+exclamation point (!)
Create or edit a hyperlink.	Ctrl+K
Check spelling in the active worksheet or selected range.	F7
Display the Quick Analysis options for selected cells that contain data.	Ctrl+Q
Display the Create Table dialog box.	Ctrl+L or Ctrl+T

Work With Data, Functions, And The Formula Bar: Keyboard Shortcuts.

TASK	SHORTCUT
Select an entire PivotTable report.	Ctrl+Shift+asterisk (*)
Edit the active cell and put the insertion point at the end of its contents. Or, if editing is turned off for the cell, move the insertion point into the formula bar. If editing a formula, toggle Point mode off or on so you can use arrow	F2

keys to create a reference.	
Expand or collapse the formula bar.	Ctrl+Shift+U
Cancel an entry in the cell or Formula Bar.	Esc
Complete an entry in the formula bar and select the cell below.	Enter
Move the cursor to the end of the text when in the formula bar.	Ctrl+End
Select all text in the formula bar from the cursor position to the end.	Ctrl+Shift+End
Calculate all worksheets in all open workbooks.	F9
Calculate the active worksheet.	Shift+F9
Calculate all worksheets in all open workbooks, regardless of whether they have changed since the last calculation.	Ctrl+Alt+F9
Check dependent formulas, and then calculate all cells in all open workbooks, including cells not marked as needing to be calculated.	Ctrl+Alt+Shift+F9
Display the menu or message for an Error Checking button.	Alt+Shift+F10
Display the Function Arguments dialog box when the insertion point is to the right of a function name in a	Ctrl+A

formula.	
Insert argument names and parentheses when the insertion point is to the right of a function name in a formula.	Ctrl+Shift+A
Invoke Flash Fill to automatically recognize patterns in adjacent columns and fill the current column	Ctrl+E
Cycle through all combinations of absolute and relative references in a formula if a cell reference or range is selected.	F4
Insert a function.	Shift+F3
Copy the value from the cell above the active cell into the cell or the formula bar.	Ctrl+Shift+straight quotation mark (")
Create an embedded chart of the data in the current range.	Alt+F1
Create a chart of the data in the current range in a separate Chart sheet.	F11
Define a name to use in references.	Alt+M, M, D
Paste a name from the Paste Name dialog box (if names have been defined in the workbook.	F3
Move to the first field in the next record of a data form.	Enter
Create, run, edit, or delete a	Alt+F8

macro.	
Open the Microsoft Visual Basic For Applications Editor.	Alt+F11

Function Keys.

SHORTCUT	TASK
F1	Displays the **Excel Help** task pane. Ctrl+F1 displays or hides the ribbon. Alt+F1 creates an embedded chart of the data in the current range. Alt+Shift+F1 inserts a new worksheet.
F2	Edits the active cell and positions the insertion point at the end of the cell contents. It also moves the insertion point into the Formula Bar when editing in a cell is turned off. Shift+F2 adds or edits a cell comment. Ctrl+F2 displays the print preview area on the **Print** tab in the Backstage view.
F3	Displays the **Paste Name** dialog box. Available only if names have been defined in the workbook (**Formulas** tab, **Defined Names**

	group, **Define Name**). Shift+F3 displays the **Insert Function** dialog box.
F4	Repeats the last command or action, if possible. When a cell reference or range is selected in a formula, F4 cycles through all the various combinations of absolute and relative references. Ctrl+F4 closes the selected workbook window. Alt+F4 closes Excel.
F5	Displays the **Go To** dialog box. Ctrl+F5 restores the window size of the selected workbook window.
F6	Switches between the worksheet, ribbon, task pane, and Zoom controls. In a worksheet that has been split (**View** menu, **Manage This Window**, **Freeze Panes**, **Split Window** command), F6 includes the split panes when switching between panes and the ribbon area. Shift+F6 switches between the worksheet, Zoom controls, task pane, and ribbon.

	Ctrl+F6 switches to the next workbook window when more than one workbook window is open.
F7	Displays the **Spelling** dialog box to check spelling in the active worksheet or selected range.
	Ctrl+F7 performs the **Move** command on the workbook window when it is not maximized. Use the arrow keys to move the window, and when finished press Enter, or Esc to cancel.
F8	Turns extend mode on or off. In extend mode, **Extended Selection** appears in the status line, and the arrow keys extend the selection.
	Shift+F8 enables you to add a nonadjacent cell or range to a selection of cells by using the arrow keys.
	Ctrl+F8 performs the **Size** command (on the **Control** menu for the workbook window) when a workbook is not maximized.
	Alt+F8 displays the **Macro** dialog box to create, run, edit, or delete a macro.
F9	Calculates all worksheets in all open

	workbooks. Shift+F9 calculates the active worksheet. Ctrl+Alt+F9 calculates all worksheets in all open workbooks, regardless of whether they have changed since the last calculation. Ctrl+Alt+Shift+F9 rechecks dependent formulas, and then calculates all cells in all open workbooks, including cells not marked as needing to be calculated. Ctrl+F9 minimizes a workbook window to an icon.
F10	Turns key tips on or off. (Pressing Alt does the same thing.) Shift+F10 displays the shortcut menu for a selected item. Alt+Shift+F10 displays the menu or message for an Error Checking button. Ctrl+F10 maximizes or restores the selected workbook window.
F11	Creates a chart of the data in the current range in a separate Chart sheet.

	Shift+F11 inserts a new worksheet.
	Alt+F11 opens the Microsoft Visual Basic For Applications Editor, in which you can create a macro by using Visual Basic for Applications (VBA).
F12	Displays the **Save As** dialog box.

Other Useful Shortcut Keys

SHORTCUT	TASK
Alt	Displays the Key Tips (new shortcuts) on the ribbon. For example, Alt, W, P switches the worksheet to Page Layout view. Alt, W, L switches the worksheet to Normal view. Alt, W, I switches the worksheet to Page Break Preview view.
Arrow Keys	Move one cell up, down, left, or right in a worksheet. Ctrl+Arrow Key moves to the edge of the current data region in a worksheet. Shift+Arrow Key extends the

	selection of cells by one cell. Ctrl+Shift+Arrow Key extends the selection of cells to the last nonblank cell in the same column or row as the active cell, or if the next cell is blank, extends the selection to the next nonblank cell. Left Arrow or Right Arrow selects the tab to the left or right when the ribbon is selected. When a submenu is open or selected, these arrow keys switch between the main menu and the submenu. When a ribbon tab is selected, these keys navigate the tab buttons. Down Arrow or Up Arrow selects the next or previous command when a menu or submenu is open. When a ribbon tab is selected, these keys navigate up or down the tab group. In a dialog box, arrow keys move between options in an open drop-down list, or between options in a group of options. Down Arrow or Alt+Down Arrow opens a selected drop-down list.
Backspace	Deletes one character to the left in the Formula Bar.

	Also clears the content of the active cell.
	In cell editing mode, it deletes the character to the left of the insertion point.
Delete	Removes the cell contents (data and formulas) from selected cells without affecting cell formats or comments.
	In cell editing mode, it deletes the character to the right of the insertion point.
End	End turns End mode on or off. In End mode, you can press an arrow key to move to the next nonblank cell in the same column or row as the active cell. End mode turns off automatically after pressing the arrow key. Make sure to press End again before pressing the next arrow key. End mode is shown in the status bar when it is on.
	If the cells are blank, pressing End followed by an arrow key moves to the last cell in the row or column.
	End also selects the last command on the menu when a menu or submenu is visible.

	Ctrl+End moves to the last cell on a worksheet, to the lowest used row of the rightmost used column. If the cursor is in the formula bar, Ctrl+End moves the cursor to the end of the text. Ctrl+Shift+End extends the selection of cells to the last used cell on the worksheet (lower-right corner). If the cursor is in the formula bar, Ctrl+Shift+End selects all text in the formula bar from the cursor position to the end—this does not affect the height of the formula bar.
Enter	Completes a cell entry from the cell or the Formula Bar, and selects the cell below (by default). In a data form, it moves to the first field in the next record. Opens a selected menu (press F10 to activate the menu bar) or performs the action for a selected command. In a dialog box, it performs the action for the default command button in the dialog box (the button with the bold outline, often the **OK** button).

	Alt+Enter starts a new line in the same cell.
	Ctrl+Enter fills the selected cell range with the current entry.
	Shift+Enter completes a cell entry and selects the cell above.
Esc	Cancels an entry in the cell or Formula Bar.
	Closes an open menu or submenu, dialog box, or message window.
	It also closes full screen mode when this mode has been applied, and returns to normal screen mode to display the ribbon and status bar again.
Home	Moves to the beginning of a row in a worksheet.
	Moves to the cell in the upper-left corner of the window when Scroll Lock is turned on.
	Selects the first command on the menu when a menu or submenu is visible.
	Ctrl+Home moves to the beginning of a worksheet.
	Ctrl+Shift+Home extends the

	selection of cells to the beginning of the worksheet.
Page Down	Moves one screen down in a worksheet. Alt+Page Down moves one screen to the right in a worksheet. Ctrl+Page Down moves to the next sheet in a workbook. Ctrl+Shift+Page Down selects the current and next sheet in a workbook.
Page Up	Moves one screen up in a worksheet. Alt+Page Up moves one screen to the left in a worksheet. Ctrl+Page Up moves to the previous sheet in a workbook. Ctrl+Shift+Page Up selects the current and previous sheet in a workbook.
Spacebar	In a dialog box, performs the action for the selected button, or selects or clears a check box. Ctrl+Spacebar selects an entire column in a worksheet. Shift+Spacebar selects an entire row

	in a worksheet.
	Ctrl+Shift+Spacebar selects the entire worksheet.
	• If the worksheet contains data, Ctrl+Shift+Spacebar selects the current region. Pressing Ctrl+Shift+Spacebar a second time selects the current region and its summary rows. Pressing Ctrl+Shift+Spacebar a third time selects the entire worksheet. • When an object is selected, Ctrl+Shift+Spacebar selects all objects on a worksheet.
	Alt+Spacebar displays the **Control** menu for the Excel window.
Tab	Moves one cell to the right in a worksheet.
	Moves between unlocked cells in a protected worksheet.
	Moves to the next option or option group in a dialog box.
	Shift+Tab moves to the previous cell in a worksheet or the previous option in a dialog box.
	Ctrl+Tab switches to the next tab in

	dialog box.
	Ctrl+Shift+Tab switches to the previous tab in a dialog box.

☐

Customer's Page.

This page is for customers who enjoyed Microsoft Excel 2016 Keyboard Shortcuts For Windows.

Dearly beloved customer, please leave a review behind if you enjoyed this book or found it helpful. It will be highly appreciated, thank you.

Other Books By This Publisher.

S/N	Title	Series
Series A: Limits Breaking Quotes.		
1	Discover Your Key Christian Quotes	Limits Breaking Quotes
Series B: Shortcut Matters.		
1	Windows 7 Shortcuts	Shortcut Matters
2	Windows 7 Shortcuts & Tips	Shortcut Matters
3	Windows 8.1 Shortcuts	Shortcut Matters
4	Windows 10 Shortcut Keys	Shortcut Matters
5	Microsoft Office 2007 Keyboard Shortcuts For Windows.	Shortcut Matters
6	Microsoft Office 2010 Shortcuts For Windows.	Shortcut Matters
7	Microsoft Office 2013 Shortcuts For Windows.	Shortcut Matters
Series C: Teach Yourself.		
1	Teach Yourself Computer Fundamentals	Teach Yourself
Series D: For Painless Publishing		
1	Self-Publish it with CreateSpace.	For Painless Publishing
2	Where is my money? Now solved for Kindle and CreateSpace	For Painless Publishing
3	Describe it on Amazon	For Painless Publishing
4	How To Market That Book.	For Painless Publishing

www.ingramcontent.com/pod-product-compliance
Lightning Source LLC
Chambersburg PA
CBHW070858070326
40690CB00009B/1892